Tearin' Pages Off Lost Years

Copyright ©2025 by Beatrex Quntanna
All Rights Reserved. No part of this book may be reproduced or transmitted in any form or by any means without the written permission of the publisher, except for the inclusion of brief quotations in a review.

ISBN 979-8-218-83083-0

Printed in the United States of America

ART ALA CARTE PUBLISHING

760-672-6020

beatrex8@gmail.com

www.beatrex.com

This book is dedicated to Siena Ward

Thank you to my granddaughter for her peaceful sense of spirit and bringing the birds back to my garden. It has been a wonderful, miraculous time combining our creative power together, a true blessing for the resurrection of this book from its 30-year slumber in the filing cabinet of my soul.

Table of Contents

Preface ix

1. Bein' a California Kid 11
2. The Disappointed Debutante 13
3. Bar Room Memorabilia 15
4. Sunday Mornin' Faces 17
5. It's Different This Time 19
6. Co-Star 20
7. Judgmental Eyes 21
8. A New Kind of Love 23
9. Ode to an Alcoholic 25
10. Lawyers and Ex-Husbands 26
11. Another Year Later 27
12. Tender Traces of Love 28
13. The Friday Night Wanderlust 29
14. Art ala Carte 30
15. When You Look at Me 31
16. A Tapestry Unwoven 33
17. Apathy 35
18. I Made a Wish and You Came True 37
19. Tearin' Pages Off Lost Years 39
20. A Silent, Illusive Movie 41
21. Beyond the Bounds of the Room 42
22. Both Sides 43

23. Calling Words..44
24. Feelin' Blue...45
25. Infinity at a Glance 47
26. Moonbeams..48
27. In My Defense..49
28. Double or Nothing..51
29. Prisoner—Yeah...52
30. Sensitive Simplicity.......................................55
31. Silent Soliloquy...56
32. Pretended Complacency...............................57
33. The Night of the August Moon......................58
34. September Shoreline....................................59
35. The Land of No Tomorrow............................60
36. The Marketplace of the Mind........................62
37. Watching You from Afar................................63
38. Body, Mind, Spirit...65
39. A Place Inside Laughter................................67
40. The Fourth of July in the Middle of December....................69
41. Christmas Time...71
42. What Do You Say?..73
43. Unborn Wishes and Aborted Hopes..............75
44. One Step at a Time.......................................77
Acknowledgements..78
Author..79
Other Publications & Classes 80

Bein' a California Kid

My liquid dreams turn
into high tide afternoons
while I float in this Paradise
and dream on a dune.
I'm whistlin' my favorite tune,
catchin' the glow of the sunset.
I'm burstin' with aliveness,
blowin' like a light offshore breeze,
stayin' young as long as I please,
bein' a California kid.

The Disappointed Debutante

She was born with coal black hair and had violet eyes that
had a mystical stare.
The promise of fortune and joy attached to her name;
it was Dante and Shakespeare from whence she came.

She grew up in a town that was called the Jewel,
protected with pride from all that was cruel.
She woke up every morning to the sound of the ocean;
she was allergic to mosquitoes and always wore Calamine
lotion.

She rode horses, as all good debutantes do,
her saddle was silver-studded and her horse had one eye
that was blue.
Amber was the name of the horse that she loved.
When she rode she wore chaps of white leather; they fit like
a glove.

She sailed in her boat at the yacht club too,
racing in regattas, for she was a very fine crew–
she learned very fast as all good debutants do.
Tennis became her favorite game;
when she'd miss a shot she'd belt out her name,
but that wasn't how she won her fortune and fame.

Her eyes had a sparkle that stayed with you for a while;
she lit up a room with her "genuine smile."
She learned very fast it wasn't OK to be sad,
for if she was she'd disappoint her Dad.

She grew up in a town that was called the Jewel.
Her mother taught her how to play by the rules,
so she only dated boys from very fine schools.
When she went out she always wore gloves,
prim and proper; that's the way she was.
She never let feelings get in the way;
that was a game that she didn't play.

When she was thirteen she met a boy;
he was the only one that filled her with joy.
His hair was blonde, Bill was his name.
He came from a family that knew fortune and fame.
He played tennis, sailed boats and rode horses too–
just knowing him made all of her wishes come true.
It happened one summer in a town called the Jewel;
her mother approved, you see, Stanford was the name of his school.

They were married when she was twenty,
a marriage filled with hope, for they had plenty.
She was beautiful, she walked by his side;
he was a lawyer: that filled her with pride.

They lived on a golf course and had a life filled with fun.
On her twenty-second birthday she gave birth to their son.
His hair was blonde, his eyes were blue,
he was perfect, and one more of her wishes came true.

Her second son was born in her year of twenty-four;
the year her husband got an ulcer, he couldn't take it anymore– their love became something he learned to abhor.

What happened to her beauty that walked by her side?
What happened to her lawyer that filled her with pride?
They ran from their secrets, it seemed easier to hide;
their marriage became a game that they couldn't ride.

The disappointed debutante took a look at her life–
she didn't know how to act not being his wife.
She couldn't stand the pain in her children's faces,
their shattered dreams taking them into unforeseen places.

She's examined all her wishes that didn't come true,
discovering how to work with feelings so blue.
She's sharing the feelings she wants to conceal,
and her "genuine smile" is discovering how to be real.

Bar Room Memorabilia

I see scribbled phone numbers
left on cocktail napkins,
pretended promises waiting
for something to happen.
These remains of bar room memorabilia
remind me of disco shouts that
sing, *Come on, I want to feel ya*.
A twisted fantasia of lies
borrowed in order to take,
encompassed in a kaleidoscope
of leftover lust on the make.

Sunday Mornin' Faces

I always wonder about Sunday mornin' faces
showin' up for brunch in offbeat places.
I wonder where they've been all night.
What can it be that makes them look so uptight?
My bloodshot eyes stare off into space
while drinkin' Blood Marys in this offbeat place.
I see sleepy faces snugglin' with their fantasies from
the night before,
readin' the Sunday news and watchin' the runners
gather at the door,
those long-legged men wearin' tee shirts and shorts.
Where were they last night? Did they go out and cavort?

Then there's the family who stopped in after church,
starin' at all the people they think they should convert.
Groups of guys and gals arrivin' with glimpses of yesterday
marked on their faces,
showin' up for Sunday brunch in offbeat places.
I wonder where they've been all night,
what can it be that makes them look so uptight?
Why do they go out and get all wrapped up
in the Sunday news,
when they already look like they could sing the blues?

Sunday mornin' faces fillin' themselves with omelets
covered with chili sauce,
pouring pots of coffee, drinking Bloody Marys, and
chewin' celery stalks.
Yeah – my glazed eyes stare off into space,
wonderin' why I'm here in this offbeat place,
wantin' so much to wash yesterday off my face.
I'm tryin' to forget what happened last night,
wishin' so hard I could'a made it right.
I know what it is that makes me look so uptight.
I guess I'm just one more Sunday mornin' face
showin' up for Sunday brunch in an offbeat place.

It's Different This Time

All my relationships with men start in a blaze of fire,
burning so brightly and I'm filled
with that unquenchable desire.
Then poof they're gone, and I get lost in the embers.
This leaves me with fond images and long cold
nights to remember.
It's different this time; it's a flicker of light
twinkling softly, sending sparkles that cover me with a
warmth that lasts all night.
It's not a blaze that turns my insides upside down;
it's a glowing gentle movement that keeps my feet on the
ground.

You see, once there was this dentist
who built me a shrine.
He stayed for a while, telling me stories
and drinking all my wine.
Then came the street singer who played
the harmonica in bed.
After a few weeks with him I wished I was dead.
Cupid shot the arrow one more time
in the heart of a man that told stories that rhyme.
Then came the doctor, that was really a joke;
he took off like a flash when his life went up in smoke.
So I've been alone for a while, I've been taking a rest.
My therapist advised me, she thought it was best.
Now I'm ready to know the warmth of a glow,
and my heart is singing a melody that says, *Take it slow*.
It's different this time; it's a flicker of light
twinkling softly, sending sparkles that cover me with a
warmth that lasts all night.
It's not a blaze that turns my insides upside down;
it's a glowing gentle movement that keeps my feet on the
ground.

Co-Star

I am amazed by the film I just reviewed–
it sure didn't turn out like the script I previewed.
The re-run of this one gets placed in the can
as a reminder of another unfortunate one-night stand.
Here I sit pondering with pen in my hand,
wondering when I'm going to meet up with a man
who isn't afraid to co-star with me,
and take on his part with gallantry...

Judgmental Eyes

Judgmental eyes
that rationalize
make no music with me.
Empty eyes
only criticize,
for they never learned to see.
So why should I be patronized
when loving you can't be...

A New Kind of Love

Auras of rainbows are flapping around
as I sense my soul is flying off the ground.
This rapture of movement making music in my head
dances to a beat, making a tune
out of all the wonderful words he said.
Nuances of pleasure surround my senses,
stretching my being into a whole new kind of flight,
as I recollect images of this lovely man
I was with last night.

Feelings buried so long, shoved way deep within,
are surfacing so beautifully
and walking around on the edge of my skin.
My thoughts turn into tingles as I feel
the warmth of this man,
remembering the softness of his soul
and the velvet touch of his hand.
Yes, auras of rainbows are flapping around,
awakening my senses and telling me
that a new kind of love has been found.
Yes, spirals have evolved, untangling my soul,
leading me to a wisdom that has made me surrender
to a way of loving that is so incredibly tender.

Ode to an Alcoholic

Twelve steps to sanity
are fillin' me with calamity.
I'm discoverin' who I am
through the sobriety of this man,
and I don't like what I see–
that person over there couldn't be me.

I'm hearin' about compulsion
and it's turnin' into revulsion,
seein' who I am,
wonderin' if I give a damn.

I'm learnin' about obsession
hearin' this man's confession
about a life he drank away,
and I'm wonderin' if I can play.

Twelve steps to sanity
are fillin' me with calamity.
I'm discoverin' who I am
through the sobriety of this man,
and I don't like what I see–
that person over there couldn't be me.

Seein' who I am, hearin' stories about drinkin',
is makin' my mind do too much thinkin'.
I'm takin' inventory
listenin' to this man's story,
hearin' things I don't want to hear
is makin' my path way too clear.

I know about compulsion
and it's turnin' into revulsion,
seein' who I am
through the sobriety of this man,
and I don't like what I see–
that person over there couldn't be me.

Lawyers and Ex-Husbands

The man in the pin-striped suit
had a manner I found most crude.
He invaded my space as an
unwelcome visitor from my past,
the kind of being I thought I was rid of at last.
A form of personage, packaged so perfectly, loaded
with pretense so it looks as if he can perform.
What the package says to me is all he does is conform.
Pin-stripes and Glen plaid, three pieces designed to make
him look dignified,
so that his clients can feel satisfied,
and the bills he sends, justified.

Another Year Later

It's another year later on the fourth of July.
I still delight in my fantasy of you, I can't tell you why.
I wonder if you'd remember that moment in time
when you jumped over the sea wall
and turned into a rhyme–
a stanza of words written on parchment paper,
cemented by an illusion that is still real one year later.

Tender Traces of Love

I was buyin' a can of tennis balls with a man I adore,
wearin' tennis whites, and standin' in a store.
I was foolin' with my wallet, waitin' for my change,
smilin' into my lover's face when I saw something
very strange–

ruby red lips perfectly placed on his cheeks
glaring back at me,
tender traces of love left on his face
for the whole world to see,
like footprints in the sand, one right after the other–
as soon as I'd wipe one off, I would find another.

The Friday Night Wanderlust

I'm sick of seeing frozen faces
showin' up in forgotten places.
I'm sick of watching bodies shuffle
through a human turnstile of hope,
as they wander aimlessly towards plastic dreams.

I'm sick of hearin' stories that have been told before
and lookin' at eyes that are always searchin' for more.
They're comin' to see how much life they can steal,
grabbing onto a glory ride they want to be real,
holdin' on so tight.

I'm sick of watchin' my frolic of fantasy
deteriorate and crumble into dust,
in the never ending search for the Friday Night Wanderlust.

Art ala Carte

My desk is piled high with papers stuck between
ash trays filled with cigarette butts.
The weeks wiz by, marked by a calendar of stale coffee
left in paper cups.
Stacks of paintings are filed on the floor–
it's so bad on most days you can't get through the door.
The sound of the staple gun blasts from the back room
while the compressor gurgles its favorite tune.
The phone rings so loud that it shakes off the wall.
A gal in French braids monitors the calls
for the lady wearing silk stockings,
looking as pretty as can be.
I mumble in the background,
wondering why the phone is never for me.

When You Look at Me

As you dissect parts of my soul, I wonder what you see,
when you look at me.
The scanning ray of your vision moves like a telescope;
the lenses of your eyes are like a microscope,
peeling off the layers that you see,
when you look at me.

The piercing placement of your eyes upon my heart
comes at me with such clarity,
darting so directly, searching for my sincerity.
To know the feel of such a glance is quite a rarity–
often I feel frightened and wonder what you see,
when you look at me.

A Tapestry Unwoven

You are to me a tapestry unwoven,
and I the threads that were not chosen.
You are to me a symphony unplayed,
and I the notes waiting in silence, totally dismayed.
I wonder, if an earthquake placed us on a
drifting piece of land corralled by the sea,
if you could see beyond your blindfolded
illusion, and face the reality of me?

Apathy

I'm left standing all wrapped up,
packaged in painful tears.
Familiar moments of darkness cover
this empty silence I've been standing in for years.
The hollow in my heart resounds with confusion,
as shattered rainbows break slowly into faltered illusion.
Never to shine again, the rainbow's arch
has fallen and its brilliance fades away,
completing the cycle and taking its light from day.
Painfully my vision sees beyond time,
moving through distance,
proclaiming a knowing that I can't move
beyond this resistance.
My heart doesn't know how to work
when it has to be persistent,
so it closes silently, shattering rainbows
right out of existence.
You see I'd rather be all wrapped up,
packaged in painful tears,
having familiar moments of darkness cover
this empty silence I've been standing in for years.

I Made a Wish and You Came True

Our relationship started with *I love you*,
and through the beauty and perfection of that start,
there is nothing left to do. I made a wish and you came
true, and sadness comes up because there is nothing
left to do.

It started with flowers and champagne and a walk
on the beach–
you were there with me and there was no need to
campaign or make a speech. All there was that night
was you and me in the glory of our creation, the sun,
the surf and the sand. It was the birth of something
special, so perfect was that night– it was as if we were
sitting in God's hand.

Our relationship started on that night with *I love you*,
and through the beauty and perfection of that night
there is nothing left to do. I made a wish and you came
true, and sadness comes up because there is nothing
left to do.

Here I sit alone and sad and filled with pain, and saying
I love you sounds so mundane when what I really want
to do is be with you.
I know how well you'll say that I'm insane,
as I sit here remembering flowers and champagne,
wanting so much to recreate that night with you,
that night I made a wish and you came true,
and such sadness comes up because there is nothing
left to do.

Tearin' Pages Off Lost Years

She wore red shoes,
walkin' proud like front page news.
She was alive in her manner,
oozin' with glamour,
dressed in fine red silk,
sewn together like a patch-work quilt.
She was wearin' her million dollar smile
that sparkled with its own kinda style,
while she danced to old-time songs
in a place she used to belong.
She was tearin' pages off lost years,
removin' time's lied-to fears,
seein' faces from the lost and found,
standin' on old familiar ground,
comin' home to a comfort she forgot she knew,
facin' feelin's that were long overdue.
She was watchin' changed similarities
through eyes that come from clarity,
takin' life's gift of rarity
and lovin' it momentarily.
Wearin' red shoes,
feelin' proud like front page news.
She was tearin' pages off lost years,
findin' joy instead of tears,
comin' home to a comfort she forgot she knew,
finally facin' feelin's that were long overdue.

A Silent, Illusive Movie

The crescent moon sways as it holds
the forbidden fruit of my fantasy,
turning a galaxy of dreams into a lost legacy
that shines bright violet, pulsating with possibility.
I swing on this sliver of a moon,
hanging by a silver spiraled thread,
woven by twilight's sparkle, twisted by moonbeams
that turn into a reality I dread.

Why must I be hypnotized by your violet light
hanging in the hollow of my heart,
enchanted in a neverland of ideal dreams
that end before they start.

My fantasy of you rides on a pilgrimage of seduction,
isolated in a silent illusive movie
that has become my midnight production.

I awaken to confusion that's born anew
with the dawning of each day,
wondering why we can't expand beyond the horizon
of illusion and capture the milky way...

Beyond the Bounds of the Room

My words, pronounced perfectly,
echoed in the microphone,
vibrating venerable verses
presented to you alone.
We touched on a secret level
that was deep and very personal
in a setting that was all too commercial.
Under the guise of love universal
we went into another dimension,
beyond the bounds of comprehension,
isolated inside words that rhyme,
and I surrounded you with my feelings
that get better, marked by the seasons of time...

Both Sides

There are two sides to our friendship:
one that bellows, removing the bounds of time
and walks an unknown distance on the road
eternally sublime.

On the other side of our friendship
a coldness exists, beyond the comfort zone,
and I'm struck by a stranger that brings on
the awareness of my being alone.

Calling Words

What is it like to live with fear?
It becomes the distant song of calling words
that seem so near.
High tide is pulled by the moon's power.
Trembling waves rumble within me by the hour,
tossing and turning like high tide.
That's what it's like to have fear by your side.

It stretches my senses into waiting and wondering.
Knowing what a cloud feels like before thundering
is like an awakening suspended in time, pulled way inside.
Fear is an audacious movement that takes me
for a very bumpy ride.
It becomes the distant song of calling words that
seem so near–
that's what it's like to live with fear.

Feelin' Blue

I watched T.V. tonight and saw the dream of illusion
that comes out of Hollywood creating such confusion.
Seeing fairy tales come alive on the screen, right
before my eyes, makes real living so difficult when
I've been programmed by so many lies.
During each show the prince falls for the princess,
they unite so beautifully and turn into Mr. and Mrs.
I see the crime in watching T.V.
and seeing a life portrayed that never can be.
It destroys the innocence of youth
and makes them think real life is uncouth.
As I turn away from the screen
and take a look at where I've been,
I see the crime it is to have believed in stories so untrue–
no wonder I've been feeling so incredibly blue.

Infinity at a Glance

I look into your eyes and see infinity;
as you look back at me I wonder what it can be.
Our eyes match each other in depth, you know,
they reflect images floating far beyond
any place I ever go.
It happens on a bridge of light, passing through
a tunnel of time,
drifting on the warping thought that always
seems to rhyme.

How come I still see infinity at a glance,
when the mirrors of our souls come together
for a millisecond dance?
In a flicker of light I see that time can stop,
racing down a rainbow that has been so carefully locked.
Infinity to reality paved with a rainbow for a road
with a light flashing like a beacon,
bouncing off the tunnel as it glows.

When I look at you and you look back at me,
I go to a place that I call infinity.
Somehow I always find my way back to reality.
I wonder how, after all this time, it can be,
that when I look into your eyes I always see infinity?
Dancing on a bridge of light, passing through
a tunnel of time,
drifting on a warping thought that always
seems to rhyme,
seeing a rainbow that we never took
the time to climb.

Moonbeams

Satin softness lingers in my trance
left by the shooting star.
Moonbeams line the distance marking the
place where I am and where you are.
They are twinkling on a lineage of time,
floating down an avenue of trust,
taking their brilliance and transforming
it into gold dust.

Last night I saw a shooting star sprinkling
softly into a bold new reality, blocked by a hollow door.
I couldn't find my way through the bright labyrinth
lights, fearing that I'd lost you once more.
Even though the moonbeams mark the place,
showing me where you are,
I find it hard to know what to wish for when I see a
shooting star.

In My Defense

I care about the sound and rhythm in words.
I hear a cadence in the way they should be heard.
Melodies without music should be spoken in
order to captivate,
if mouthed perfectly they should punctuate,
precisely pronounced, producing precision.
I like speaking in a way that gives words rhythm.

Double or Nothing

The roll is a high one, double or nothing I say–
the stakes are too real and I don't want to play.
There is a goddess who knows from way deep inside
that this is one game where I can't hide.
I want to run and not have to wait.
I Ching says don't go out of the gate.
The seed has been planted, you watch it grow–
this time you don't get to let go.
The growth is too slow and I don't want to wait.
Certainty, I shout from myself as I pull out my hair.
It was so much easier when I didn't care.
It seems so easy to go run and hide
and never have anyone to stand by my side.
The roll is a high one, double or nothing I say–
the stakes are too real and I don't want to play.

Prisoner — Yeah

Yeah — I was locked up in jail,
I was beggin' you to put up the bail.
I was holdin' onto everything in sight,
especially you, reachin' out
and grabbin' you so tight.
I was watchin' my world go down the drain,
sittin' on the inside all locked up,
watchin' the rain,
so afraid I'd get wet.

My definitions were defined, my rituals
were safe,
grabbin' onto what I thought was real,
holdin' on so tight.
My survival was at stake, so I shut the door
where I thought it was safe.

Two weeks past, I went way inside
where it's as cold as ice.
My Emily Post came back, my woman
went away,
and my "little girl" didn't want to play.
My kids saw no love, their dog died
and they got to be right.
Those two weeks were a cold empty night.

Yeah — I was in jail,
and there was no one to put up the bail.
There was no warmth to my tears–
those two weeks were years.
I was grabbin' at reality,
playin' with congeniality
and cursin' immortality.

Choosin' is the only way to decide,
said a voice from way inside.
Get out, you don't need to run and hide,
so I saw my way to the other side.

I wanted to get out of jail,
so I put up the bail.
I left congeniality behind and saw
there is no reality that isn't mine.
I'm on my way to discover my
own immortality,
and the one thing that comes up is,
I don't want to define...

Sensitive Simplicity

You touch me with the softness of feathers,
arousing my senses into a myriad of pleasures,
filling my body with complete delight
and sending the essence of me way beyond sight.
The sensitive simplicity of your nature fills the hollow
in my heart that has only known emptiness,
complicating the facets of my kaleidoscope soul
lined in velvet readiness.

Silent Soliloquy

Distant electricity diminishes my
soul in search of warm closeness.
Reality stands still and spreads my
being into paper-thin hopelessness,
like liquid cellophane, transparent
in its fluidity.

I transpose my soul across the sky
and stand silent in my soliloquy,
stunned as I watch the essence of my
feelings crystalize and turn to stone,
like prisms that need to catch their light,
for they have none of their own.

Pretended Complacency

Our inner galactic connection
causes solitary introspection,
blockaded by my fear of rejection.
Still, I wait in pretended complacency,
pondering monumental layers
of bewildered expectancy,
propelling inside-out, confused
from watching a fading essence
of possibility diffuse.

The Night of the August Moon

It was the night of the August moon when she
painted the town;
she took my whole life and turned it around.
She had a story to tell about a man we shared;
she had a message of truth for all those who cared.
She painted my car and my office too;
she called on the phone and said, *He's untrue*.

She painted the town the night of the August moon,
and what I want her to know is we'll get her soon.
The story she told hasn't ended yet;
the message of truth is the lesson to get.

She delivered the story, not just to me:
she made sure I knew the number was three.
She painted their cars and their offices, too.
When she started a fire I asked, *What else can she do*?

The moon is in August and she still comes
without a sound;
she took my whole life and turned it around.
She has a story to tell that really has me scared,
and what I discovered is how much I've cared.
I thank her for letting me know there are three,
and what I want her to know is that it doesn't bother me.
She took my whole life and turned it around,
and the lesson for me is to stand my ground.

September Shoreline

Hollow echoes haunt
the September Shoreline
in a silence familiar to
my melancholy mind.
The unfulfilled promise
of summer fades into mist
and collects in sculptured pockets
etched in the sides of the cliffs,
vaporizing into lost dimensions
that were never allowed to exist.
This lonely barren beach resounds with
sounds of hollow rhythmic breathing,
void in a vacant vacuum, waiting
for the changing of the season.

The Land of No Tomorrow

I'll tell you about the game of easy come, easy go–
it's a game I don't want to know.
I'll hold up and talk to you.
I'll tell you what I'm gonna do.
I've found the dream at the end of the rainbow.
My light knows where to go.
I know what I'm gonna do–
I'm gonna walk upwards with you.
That's how it's gonna be, walking through reality,
crossing to the other side of immortality,
to a place I've never been before–
    a place that only knows an open door;
    a place where we can hide and find time to explore;
    a place where we can move only as far as we can see;
    a place where acceptance is the key.
The vision I have has no form and there is nothing to borrow,
we own our own joy and we own our own sorrow–
that's the way it is in the land of no tomorrow.
It's not a game of easy come, easy go–
that's the game I don't want to know.
Come with me to the end of the rainbow.
Follow the light with me, it knows where to go.

Come, walk upwards with me,
to the land of no tomorrow, where the door is
always open and acceptance is the key.

The Marketplace of the Mind

I.
Words that erupt from a feeling within
are always received with a knowing of where they have been.
Receiving words transmitted by thought
are delivered so carefully as if they were to be bought.
It saddens me to see the marketplace of the mind,
where pictures are painted with words as if they were to be sold to the blind.
Simplicity is all it takes to deliver a message that is real,
all anyone needs to do is give himself permission to feel.

II.
What a rarity it is to find a heart that is not blocked.
It seems as if all people's hearts have been sold or hocked.
A decision is made that comes out of rage,
and our hearts become blocked at a very early age.
I find it hard to fathom that all people's hearts are gone
and that human life is being sold for a song.
What happened to the days when people had souls?
Have they given them up as they race toward their goals?
I find it hard to cultivate my life this way
with feelings milling around that I can't say.
The eruption that wells from way deep inside
tells me that my heart doesn't want to hide.
Yet cowardice takes over and covers up what's real,
and truth becomes something that is hard to reveal.
I see how easy it is for one to sell out,
and being one who sees the truth I even begin to doubt.
I need to find a space that is brilliantly bold
where all of my feelings can be honestly be told.

Watching You from Afar

It was a wonderful party, I delighted in watching you from afar, ambling around your garden, acting like a movie star.

You gave me a gardenia to wear in my hair,
a simple gift of friendship to show me that you care.
Its soft scented fragrance lingered lusciously around my face, shifting in and out like a cool breeze flows through Chantilly lace, being ever present and suddenly leaving without a trace.

Yes, it was a wonderful party, I marveled as I watched you laugh with friends under surprised Del Dios trees, inviting them to bask in the cool afternoon breeze. Rancho Delux was filled with your ever present pride, flowing with a magnetic energy that ripples through the wind and comes as does the tide.

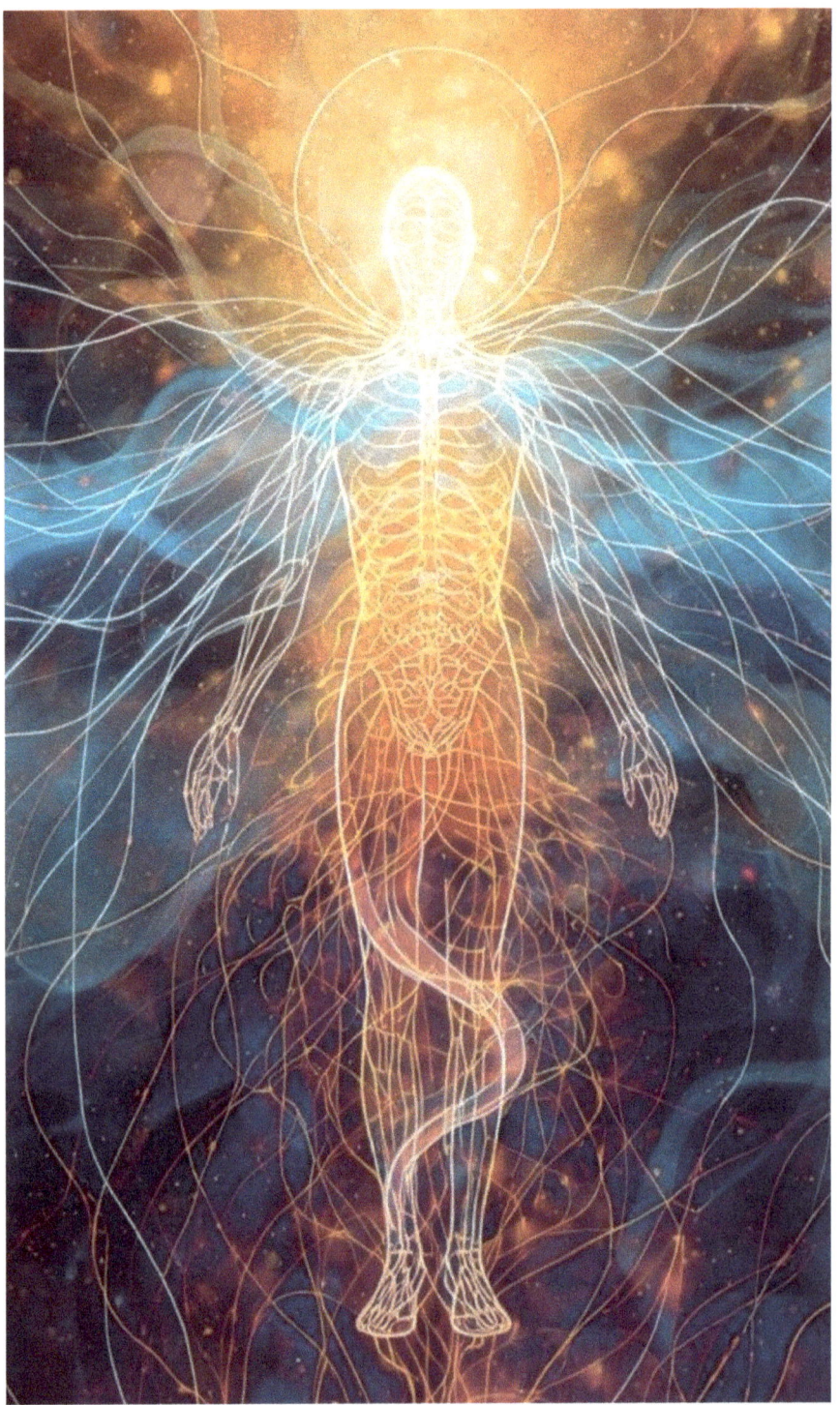

Body, Mind, Spirit

Body
I pay homage to fire energy
that darts with electricity,
flowing in the form of infinity,
incapsulated in my body,
declaring it open space,
propelled by a force that
I'm now able to face.

Mind
My visual perceptions personify
passion and placate past pictures
that burn negatives of life gone by,
transposing new experiences presented
playfully by life's process and promise.

Spirit
Sculptured solitude solidifies
silence that speaks in a soft voice,
awakening my senses that metamorphose
into the reality of choice.

A Place Inside Laughter

I have walked alone for many years
drenched in the stains of my unforgotten tears.
I have marched around corners of a maniacal maze
trapped by the past darkness of my pent-up rage.
I have felt the echoing shrills of death,
not knowing if the next day would give me breath.
I have prided myself by suffering unsurmountable pain,
not knowing if I could untangle life's untwistable chain,
searching endlessly for a place inside laughter
where my loved one and I would stay forever after.
Then spirals evolved, lifting me into a softer space,
untangling my soul and placing me above life's
untwistable race.
A celebration filtered in with its laser beam light,
removing the stains from my darkest night.
I'm soaring into a place that has no time,
beyond dreams where laughter is born and
bubbles into vintage wine.
I'm frolicking inside softness, all wrapped up
in his abundant arms,
captured graciously, lifted by love's alluring charms.

The Fourth of July in the Middle of December

It was the fourth of July, he was big and tall.
I noticed him as he ran towards the beach
and jumped over the sea wall.
His hair was blond, his shorts were navy blue;
I watched him carefully as he laughed with friends,
that's all I could do.
His smile was real, his attitude robust,
his energy was gentle; he seemed to be a man
I could trust.

He whistled Christmas carols as we shopped for presents
and walked through the mall.
He moves very fast for a man so tall.
We stopped for pizza and over a liter of wine,
I told him the truth and laid my heart on the line.
How easy that is when there is nothing to lose.
He laughed in amazement as he said, *I get to choose.*
So I'm left with a picture of a man blonde and tall
who ran smack into my life as he jumped over a sea wall.

Christmas Time

Christmas time,
drinkin' wine,
rememberin' a story
that once had glory,
feelin' sublime
about a story so divine.

Rediscoverin' December
as a time to be tender.
While the fire turns to ember,
I drink wine
and reflect on Christmas time.

My anxiety seems low;
no one's telling me where to go.
I finally learned how to receive
the joy of Christmas eve.

I remember pushin' so hard
when I forgot the brightness of the star
that tells the Christmas story,
the one about glory.

I remember bein' so tired
gettin' things ready for those who desired,
never rememberin' to think of me
or ever feelin' that could be.

I know the story is about carin'
to take time for sharin'.
That's the way it is now–
thank you God I finally learned how.

Sittin' back feelin' sublime
rememberin' Christmas time,
reflectin' all those images
of when I was worse than the Grinches,
when all I thought of was greed–
I couldn't even remember the Apostle's Creed.

Nothing was right.
I was always uptight
whenever it was Christmas night,
worryin' and wonderin' what I would get,
keepin' my children in constant upset.

Now all that is gone.
I know a new Christmas song.
I finally know where I belong,
sittin' back drinkin' wine,
lovin' that it's Christmas time,

rememberin' a story
that still has glory,
feelin' sublime
knowing a story so divine–
thank you God for Christmas time.

What Do You Say?

People say I should give you up, you know.
They say a year has gone by and I need to let go.
It hurts to hear the words they say,
to know we won't be together someday.

My psychic says you are part of the plan,
and a day will come when we'll walk hand in hand.
My heart tells me there is hope for us–
I need to be patient and learn to trust.
My mind says I'm playing a fool's game,
that fantasy and reality are not the same.

What do you say?

Unborn Wishes and Aborted Hopes

My wishes glow brightly and dance above my fireplace.
They wrap around me in a strangling way, squeezing out an emotion that I'm unable to face.
Hoping twirls and twists into a glittery emotional design; as it looks me in the eyes I discover a feeling I'm unable to define.
Hopes and wishes come together and march on my hearth, prancing in cadence, as if they were in a parade.
The beat of their marching has a definite statement to make. It says,
Follow me once more for old times sake.

Oh, how pretty they look spangled by the glitter they spark, marching in a parade of disappointed memories, cavorting on a stage for me to look at in the dark.
Hope goes by me, gallantly stepping and strutting as if to say, *Follow me and everything will go your way.*

Wishing comes softly, swishing and swirling and singing a Siren's tune:
If you come with me I'll make it better soon.

The beckoning call of wishes and hopes draws me closer to the warmth of the fire.
The comfort zone they try to create sends chills that echo into the empty cavern of my desires.
They crystallize in front of me as I remember all the places they said they'd take me on a whim.
Unborn wishes and aborted hopes resound in my head, as I remember all the unforgotten dreams and places I've never been.

One Step at a Time

I'm walking on a whole new ground, earth just created, never been stepped on before. My footprints touch this earth with apprehension as they feel their way, not knowing which avenue to explore.

I am a vessel of truth, exposed, having nothing to hide. Created before me is a movement of energy, I know not how to ride. The absence of wisdom and knowledge brings on uncertainty that leads my mind astray and makes an awesome awareness of my power come into play.

This beginning is like the dawn that doesn't know how to bring on the day. It's a movement in nature daring to stand still, demanding a push to take the pain away. I'm riding a crest of a wave that's bringing me into a land of newness I know nothing about, presenting me with a pre-arranged plan I can't see, delaying my reaction and filling me with doubt.

I'm not knowing how to walk one step at a time, one foot planted on this whole new earth and then the other, and I'm so scared of this new beginning, wondering what secrets it will uncover.

Acknowledgements

Special thanks to Donna Dircz for her dedication to these poems. She lovingly transcribed them and gave them new life by creating the perfect visual images for the continuation of my story.

Thank you to Siena Ward for her persistence and commitment to getting this project done in the true spirit of the Poetry Muse who dances together in us. She is a very thorough editor and inspirational granddaughter.

As always, a big thank you to Catherine Renshon for her ability to capture art forms within her own creative structure. Her editorial layout helped bring this work to life!

Beatrex Quntanna

Beatrex Quntanna was raised in La Jolla, California. She woke up to the sound of the ocean and experienced the wonders and fantasies of love through collecting seashells, making sandcastles and dreaming about princes.

She acted in the Old Globe Theatre in 1963 during the Shakespearian Festival, and that is where she discovered the power of performance and the joy of applause. She went on to study at the Pasadena Playhouse School of Theatre Arts. She was married in 1966 and had two beautiful children, William and Christopher Dougherty. Following a separation from her husband, she began her life as a full-time artist. It was at this time that she wrote *Tearin' Pages Off Lost Years*. This would not be the end of her colorful career which led her all over the world, lecturing and teaching the practice of metaphysics and spiritual living.

Love is a principle, not a practice. Remember to Live Love Everyday! -Beatrex

Other Publications by Beatrex

To order, go to www.beatrex.com or call 1-760-944-6020

LIVING BY THE LIGHT OF THE MOON

The Annual Moon Book and corresponding calendar is a must-have for lovers of the Moon! Honor the year of the FIRE HORSE with this 28th edition.

Living by the Light of the Moon workbook will create magic and abundance in your life! This annual workbook will show you how to navigate your life by the light of the Moon and its cycles, release what you need to shed, and manifest what you truly want.

Our video class series helps you understand how to use the workbook easily and effortlessly.
The course includes:

• High-quality instructional videos on each aspect of the book.

• A handout that makes it easy to follow along.

• And the warmth and wisdom of Beatrex to carry you on your journey.

You can also join us in community for our bi-monthly Moon Class on Zoom!

TAROT: A UNIVERSAL LANGUAGE

Embark on this fascinating journey through the unfolding Story of Life as told by the Universal Language of the Tarot. This book contains innovative avenues to understand the tarot through symbology. It includes an interpretation of all 78 Tarot cards and readings created by this nationally-known Tarot teacher, reader, and symbolist.

Plus, take the online course for more in-depth instruction. Beatrex has over forty-three years of experience giving Tarot readings and teaching the Tarot to her students.

- Get to know the meanings and symbols of the Tarot.
- Strengthen your intuition using the cards.
- Receive custom reading spreads.
- Learn to set up a vortex in your office for readings.
- Understand how to care for and treat your Tarot deck.

The course includes high-quality instructional videos, study aids, fun quizzes, and insightful activities. Whether you are on a journey to learn the Tarot for your own enlightenment or whether you want to do Tarot card readings for others, this is the course for you.

Beatrex fills the course with her insightful wisdom, funny stories, and deep, anchored knowledge of the Tarot.

You can also join us in community on the third Sunday of each month for our Sunday Tarot course on Zoom!

www.ingramcontent.com/pod-product-compliance
Lightning Source LLC
Chambersburg PA
CBHW040304170426
43194CB00021B/2893